Allen Ginsberg in the sixties

"On May, 7, 1965, Irwin Allen Ginsberg, American poet, born June 3, 1926, in New Jersey in the U.S.A." was expelled from Czechoslovakia. The organ of the Czechoslovakian Writers' Association, *Literarni noviny*, called him "the most unusual representative of non-academic American poetry whose poems are already known to our readers" and quoted him:

> When we set out to write a novel or a poem or to paint a picture, we have no idea of the outcome of the process. The concept of a creative plan is alien to us. It would therefore be difficult for me to be an artist in an environment where art has a specific programme and where an ideology prevails. I try to grasp the world without labels, categories or ideology — only with an open mind.

Brought up as a Communist Jew, Ginsberg is in the major American tradition of anarchism — Thoreau's "majority of one". Writing in *Literarni noviny* number twelve, Igor Hajek wrote:

> Ginsberg is a large blackbird standing on one leg and listening until the music of life reveals itself to him . . . and whose visit reminds us that the complexity of the world does not allow us to close our eyes to any human problem.

In his shabby clothes and tennis shoes, Ginsberg became a figure in Prague, the very embodiment of the revolutionary poet in any totalitarian society — capitalist, fascist or communist. Therefore during the *Majales* he was popularly crowned King of the May in honour of his clear rejuvenatory anarchic powers. (see "Kral Majales", *Planet News*, 1968) Since, to the police in any systematic state, he would represent freedom, he was arrested and the organ of offical youth, *Mlada fronta*, attacked both his morality and Hajek's article. Ginsberg's diary was quoted to prove his sexual licentiousness, his criticism of communism, and his hostility to any signs that human lives were being manipulated for any reason:

> One evening among close friends in Prague he sang a panegyric to the monarchy and pleaded for its re-establishment. His mastery of paradox, well-aimed aphorisms and sophistries, impulsiveness and unconventional life won him a large audience of young companions in Prague who followed his free-ranging intuition as if bewitched by the pipes of Marsyas. [1]

As Klingenberg observes, his violation of "the explicit and tacit canons of a foreign guest's behaviour" was open and obvious. But that has been the necessary operation of the western romantic poet at least since Blake and Shelley, both of whom stand in Ginsberg's pantheon, as much for their anarchism as for their legislative poetry and its political motivations.

But the anarchist position is notoriously difficult to maintain without it degenerating into a crude iconoclasm, the mirror image of the crude authoritarianism of the world it opposes, equally simplistic and equally intolerant. Ginsberg has generally been able to avoid this because he has the intelligence of his body's convictions for freedom. There was a time when he could be a manically disintegrative power on those open to his energy — Carl Solomon records his submission and opposition in those passages of *Mishaps, Perhaps* which concern their relationship, in and out of the New York Psychiatric Institute, in 1949. The two young men sustained a state of mutual hallucination in order to become real:

---

[1] E. Klingenberg: Ginsberg's Czech Expulsion — *Censorship*, 3, Summer 1965.

2

Shortly after my mummification and defiance of Amenhotip, I encountered what appeared to be a new patient, to whom I mumbled amiably, "I'M KIRILOV". He mumbled in reply "I'M MYSHKIN". The cadence of the superreal was never challenged; not one of us would dare assume responsibility for a breach of the unity which each hallucination required.

And later:

Dear Allen:

YOMOLKA and all I have escaped from the lunatic rathole which your perverted old auntie antics drove me into. [2]

Only recently has Ginsberg been able to shake off hallucinatory relationships with his followers and audiences; his prophetic power is now clear of the early Beat image — necessary in its anarchic programme of projective verse and exhibitionist nakedness, but insufficiently explicit in its political and psychological aims. The Beat had a violent freshness which barely concealed a suicidal retreat into self-exploration and cosmic consciousness. Ginsberg created himself as a laboratory of experiment for the expanded consciousness out of an experience of poetry, religion and drugs. Within that search lay the hunt for an adequate decision on what the term 'God' could mean for him; that is, his energy has been directed towards a definition of power in the self, by the self and beyond the self. Although this has meant a fusion of a great deal of information, there is little sign that Ginsberg has a manic desire for epic grandeurs; John Clellon Holmes is exaggerating when he says that Ginsberg's mind operates "as if the nerves of a Rimbaud were harnessed to the immense, synthesizing vision of a Spengler".[3] The poet's vision certainly does not extend to that kind of vitalism, associated with fascism, within which Eric Bently has included Spengler.[4] He is far too conscious of his own messianic obsessions and the positions of easy oracular and charismatic leadership towards which his aims and the conditions of the world push him. A man without laws is peculiarly vulnerable to his own gifts of power.

---

[2] Carl Solomon: *Mishaps, Perhaps* 1966, pp. 36 ff. and 57.

[3] John Clellon Holmes: Nothing More to Declare, 1968 pp. 53 ff.

[4] Eric Bentley: *The Century of Hero-Worship* 1957.

"In Society" (*Underdog 8*, 1966) ends with ironic, comic self-mockery within its protest against the predations of inevitable social rounds: he shouts at some insulting woman "in a violent /and messianic voice, inspired at/last, dominating the whole room". Ginsberg wants to dominate the room but only for a purpose: the expansion and regeneration of mutual consciousness. It is the aim of his poetry, and is remote from art for its own sake or the artist's sake. His safeguard is a painful one: to be fundamentally alone and write out of that loneliness:

> Alone
> in that same self where I always was
> with Kennedy throat brain bloodied in Texas
> the television continuous blinking two radar days . . .

The rest of this poem, "November 23, 1963" (Now Now, 1965), describes the circle of friendship, which he values particularly and at which he is adept, but which is a set of contacts within which he must remain alone. He is fond of those passages in *The Tempest* where Prospero, the white magus, relinquishes the instruments of his magic power (he refers to them at the end of "The Change", for example, and in the conversation with Ernie Barry in *City Lights Journal* 2, 1964) and requests release by pardon from his audience. He once said of Elise Cowen, who typed the primary copy of "Kaddish", "she has that quality of alert solitude": it is the silent area of Allen Ginsberg himself.[5] He is acutely conscious of any movement in himself or other people towards tyranny; "A Dream" (*Gnaoua 1*, Spring 1964) gives the form of a recurring routine in his works and journals — he is an "international European city" in 1962, experiences the streets, apartments, young writers, girls with flowers, "walls pock-marked with bullet-holes", sounds of machine-gun fire. In bed with Elise Cowen he dreams of Buchenwald figures, Stalin, Roosevelt, Hitler, choruses of Russian communists, and a stroboscopically blinking death's head. But the dream ends with choruses of yellow, black and jewish people all singing: "We will have our victory!" In one of the selections from his journals in *Boss*, Summer 1966, he writes

---

5 Allen Ginsberg and Lucien Carr: Some Thoughs about Elise Cowen — *City Lights Journal 2*, 1964.

4

If I was in Power/I would also be closed in by certain/necessities of Power? No I would take/off my clothes and go naked on Television/ with Kruschev —

Nakedness and tenderness are his constant instruments of anarchic power because in this condition he is vulnerable to little of the black magic of the Faustian magus which lies inside his consciousness. In "Genocide" (*War Poems*, edited Diane di Prima, 1968) he dreams of LeRoi Jones, incarnated as an Afro-American, and laying with him, "our legs wrapped and twined round each others bodies, soft cheeks together":

He wanted to protect me in the War
storm, but was unable
for the great force that was
upon us, of strangeness and
alien white mind in America . . .

His solution to the American Dilemma, as he told Paul Carroll, is in the same belief: "my understanding is that present race hostilities is obviously frustrated relationship, frustrated love. The *ground* is desire. All hate energy is a conversion of that desire when blocked". "Kaddish", "To Aunt Rose" and "History of the Jewish Socialist Party of America" all at least partly state Ginsberg's necessary evolution out of that commitment to political party action which is a version of a more general madness threatening human lives: the organized system of manipulation. "New York to San Fran" (1965), in *Airplane Dreams: Compositions from Journals* (1968) is a meditational structure about power. The poet in a plane is in the later twentieth century area of space-time, combining movement and rest in a semi-hallucinatory journey over the Earth. Against Adlai Stevenson's Grosvenor Square death he chants the syllable of assent, "om", the sound of the universe. The sense of potential life and potential death gives way to the ironies of musical associations with the sublime and divine, heard from loudspeakers while reading newspaper headlines of the Vietnamese war. He retreats from this electronic idiocy by "breaking the 'Law'": "Hashish in the Bathroom". But the euphoria is shortlived. He watches a movie called "Spiderweb of Evil", a coincidence which might appear to be too oppressively pat but represents the kind of grim coincidence possible in modern conditions. He resists by asserting godhead in

5

himself; war on Satan, prophecy against political killers, Stalin, capitalism — in fact, the poem becomes what too often happens in Ginsberg's recent works, an hysterical and dull denunciation of the obvious: evil men of power. The music over headphones fuses the guilty land over which he passes, with its CIA, police, state prisons and scientific laboratories, with the movie which is "about the most secret chemical/warefare station on this hemisphere", and therefore "projecting/the same angst as my hashish/bathroom — /So I share in this vast fantasy /which rises like poison gas/from the man-warmed farmlands/ approaching Missouri River".

Ginsberg's theme of power and paranoia, both in himself and in his environment, is in the Sixties the centre of his concern, his vulnerability, the experience of this century. But once again the black humour of self criticism prevents egotism — "Shit the movie's attacking /us Messiahs" — and he considers the possible treasons to be committed by the Beatles, Yevtuchenko and himself, risking imprisonment. He resists paranoia in his customary way: "I must come back to my body".

It is a loose composition, compounded of associations and daft fantasies, and some of downright sloppy utterances of the worst side of Ginsberg in the Sixties, the conventional pop-bard: "It's too sad! It's too happy! /It's here, unfolding like/a giant rose . . . ". The journals are full of his manic desire to verbalize everything and the result is frequently a boring collection of anxieties and about-turns: "I'll get drunk & give no shit, / & not be a Messiah". He finishes off with a final *om* and the plane's descent. What he does not notice is that his reduction of people to broad concerns of himself is the equivalent of musak-reductiveness of movies and music in the airplane cabin. There is not sufficient rhythmic flair and language interest to fuse the experience. But then it is not a poem but a "composition". So one's criticism is not of the form so much as the sensibility of the meditation: not the messianism and counter-messianism but the reductiveness. Much the same happens in "Ankor Wat" *(Long Hair 1, 1,* 1965 and printed separately by Fulcrum Press in 1968), also called a "Composition from Journals". A letter in the *Times* Literary Supplement* for February 2, 1969, criticizes the poet's unconventional spelling of Cambodian names, and identifies the photographs in the Fulcrum edition as "probably of Ta Prohm" rather than Angkor Wat ("there is no temple of Ankor — or even of Angkor — Thom"). More important is the reduction of history to immediately personal ends at the expense of Cambodians of the past.

Ginsberg has allowed the photographs of root-entangled ruins to illustrate his poem: stone faces everywhere dislodged by roots of giant trees, and lianas splitting the smiling face of a buddha. In fact the temples of the site have long been at least partly restored to a beauty unassisted by jungle nature, and the Khmer civilization is now fairly well documented. Ginsberg's poem is about his own insecurities and anxieties in dream and social states instigated by his tourism at Angkor. It is strictly personal and blandly unhistorical. Cambodian history is ignored; we have nothing of the tyrannical king whose face smiles triumphantly in the towers, or of the slave labour which built the temples and ruined a people to the condition of weakness which made them easy prey for the Thais to the north. Inaccurate information undermines the poem's veracity. Angkor is in fact a monument to tyranny.

Yet the poem is still important for understanding Ginsberg in the Sixties, apart from this disappointing use of basic locales. His central long poems have grouped themselves into three sequences since 1956. First, "Howl", "Kaddish" "Siesta in Xbalba" and the drug poems "Laughing Gas", "Mescaline", "Lysergic Acid", "Aether", "Magic Psalm"; then, poems and compositions from the American, European and Asian journals; and thirdly, the poems which are building into the long work on "These States", an epic travel meditation on America. The Angkor poem belongs to the middle series, and "Wichita Vortex Sutra" to the last, but all Ginsberg's work is a continuous documentary of recorded experience, presented with varying degrees of relaxation and control. Part one of the Angkor poem opens with an ideogram of the penetration of roots into stone, within the gates and towers of Angkor Thom — the poet's sheltering from the rain, his fears of death, the memory of the Benares guru, Citaram, who recurs in many recent poems, who told him to "Give up desire for children" and gave him "other instructions for purity, and a passage of characteristic self-mockery of his fears of disease and death.

Curiously enough, Ginsberg does not notice that Angkor is very much an amalgam of Hindu and Buddhist faiths rather in the manner of his own synthesis. He is mainly concerned with focussing his own impressions, and much of writing has a willed, strained quality. "**Many faces in the opposite directions /in high space**" for the great towers of Angkor is simply weak. The sense of "**frail**" stone crushed by "**this modern life**" is a clear description of one aspect of the ruins — but much of this attack by vegetable life has been rectified by active restoration.

But Ginsberg is moving towards a statement of the tyrannic world which erushes into himself. He vows — once again in his recent poetry — not to eat met and "**takes refuge**" in his Self, "**the nature of my Self**" and "**my fellow Selfs**", and chants the Maha Mantra for Kali Yuga against the age of destruction. This completes the ideogram of destruction and fear of destruction.

The section ends with a passage linking his own vulnerability, the alternative he sees between highs of laughing gas or hashish and "ordering men about, playing god, without drugs", and his expedient duplicity in repeating the mudra of calm as if he were a buddha instead of "**a false Buddha afraid of /my own annihilation**", afraid of Asian violence and the paranoia of spies, telescopes and the paraphernalia of induced apprenhensiveness in our time. To reduce his panic, he makes obeisance, once again, to LeRoi Jones, the radical black poet; "**Not even afraid to be a Coward — Ashamed only by /mental voices declaring war on Darkness**".

Part two is a discussion of the politics of neutrality, followed by a characteristic self-indulgence in thoughts about war violence (this appears in most of his poetry of the Sixties), partly as a desire not simply to *read about* what he is attacking. In spite of inducements from ganja, Ta Phrom and Ta Keo yield up only a passing reference to conquering chams, fear of snakes, inhibitions about girls associated with his mother — "**a sad case of refusing to grow up give birth to die**" — and an invocation to Gary Snyder, Jack Kerouac and Robert Creeley for "answers". This is followed by a lyric conclusion in which earlier impressions of rain, roots, snakes and buddha faces are recalled while he invokes the Buddha to save him in "**this awful stone moment/ being in the streams /of change**". Ginsberg's note 15 states that "the entire text" is based on "**one night half sleeping and waking to take notes on passages in consciousness . . . made somnolent by an injection of morphine-atrophine**", while other passages are based on "**notes taken earlier that day high on ganja(pot)**".

Part three recovers a standard of interest, largely because Ginsberg is drawing attention to his compositional problems, which in themslves arise from his anarchistic attitude toward any formal authority:

> As might be read for poesy by Olson
> At least moves from perception to obsession according to waves of
> Me-ness
>   Still clinging to the Earthen straw
> My eye —

Self-doubts and sense of confusion, references to Vietnam violence, the ambivalence of soldiers and reporters towards the war, the inability of *The Outsider* to publish a poem of his on Negroes out of fear of white Southern reprisals, Pound's vow of silence, and the guru's prophecy repeated and rejected, all conclude with a final "palms together" salute to "I don't care I don't know" — a blind and undirected abandonment, under pressure, of contingent history. The final section begins by repeating earlier over-population fears, the clash of races, the possessiveness of the Earth's peoples, and the human corruption of nature instanced in a letter from Kerouac about radioactive dolphins. The poet recalls instances of energy naturally filling vacant areas, as if things cannot be opposed: there is a basic tiredness and sense of oppression in the poem: "it can/can't go on forever". In flight-dissociation over Asia, he recalls "the old elegance" of hitching a lift on earth in America and how he failed to weep at the Jerusalem wailing wall owing to confused laws "stamped /in my passport". At this crux, the tourist transcends himself into an existential traveller.

> ". . — It"
>   winds in and out of space and time the
>   physical traveller —
>   Returning home at last, years later as
> ‣   prophesied, "Is this the way that
>   I'm supposed to feel?"

His hope for clarity — "the clear air in the great Northern Mountains/and aspire to that lonely visible / Space-peak" — is crushed by a stricken conscience, and the poems ends by looking forward to the

9

calm of Kyoto: he is not ready to die, fears cowardice at death, and guesses at the nature of his own doom.

The best than can be said of such a sequence is that it is in a good anarchist tradition — Emerson and Thoreau writing up their journals into new work series. The weakness of Ginsberg's journal compositions lies in the dullness in his belabouring the American military-industrial complex and repeatedly returning to personal hang-ups. He yells at the White House, CIA, FBI, the Press, Hoover, and the rest, but they will never read him; his audiences will be snug, and perhaps smug, liberal and student listeners enjoying their righteousness. His targets are too easy, and once handled well — in "Wichita Vortex Sutra" and the tirade of "Television was a Baby Crawling Toward that Deathchamber" — there is little to be repeated with any value. Ginsberg's ability lies very much in his skill in realizing verbally the pressurized atmosphere which shapes his and our social consciousness and which escapes for nourishment to expanded consciousness. His psychic blockages and fears are also ours, which is probably why their reiteration becomes dull: fear of annihilation, the network of electronically organized conspiracies of destruction and manipulation, the energy of the cosmos taking the form of life and death illusions, nihilism and the tendency to relax into hopelessness and self-recrimination — these are the commonplaces of contemporary sensibility. It is no wonder that Kafka is constantly in his mind, the archetype of the oppressed man who knew his condition but failed to become a revolutionary in the workers' movement he believed in. In Ginsberg's case it is not the workers so much as the new generations and their musical scene — the materials of "Seabattle of Salamis Took Place off Perama" (Greek youth), "Big Beat" (a Prague pop group), "Portland Coloseum" (the Beatles), "First Party at Ken Kesey's With Hell's Angels", and "Chances 'R'".

His compositional problem is stated in a passage from the journals in *Boss*, Summer 1966: "I'll take Heisenberg for example. /the very act of writing creates emotion. But is that act sufficiently holding for the reader or hearer?" The thought process may reach "its own abstract Nothing and squiggle /of penmark symbols on Hieroglyph-paper", . . . "Ganja makes me write/ the writing seems self important/ disconnected and useless as per theory . . ." But as "Wichita Vortex Sutra" dramatizes with force and clarity, the poet's function is to recreate a language released from its national corruption, to make a white magic in the form of an "absolute contrary field" [6] against the black magic of the national system. Consciousness must be explored and widened and its rejuvenatory language invented. This is an essential part of Ginsberg's heroic action: the search for a human language in America today is itself a noble action. The Self discovers the language in itself. Discussing "The Change", Ginsberg says:

> The mind supplies the language, if you don't interfere. That's something I learned from Jack Kerouac, — how to let the mind supply the language . . . Language is a vehicle for feeling, Language itself doesn't mean anything — Wittgenstein and the Diamond Sutra agree on that. I agree with Olson that poetry is an extension of physiology. Like Tibetan Mantras, poems are an exploration of the depth of breath . . . A holy man in India told me that poetry (saddhana, which includes poetry) is also a form of Yoga discipline, because what it involves is meditation on your consciousness, awareness of your own internal universe, and, most of all, the active manifestation of the self. Sometimes the self can consciously be experienced as such . . . The discipline comes in learning how to improvise freely, how to use these rules to walk on rather than imitate from. Imitation of an earlier perception is not creation.

"The Change" concerns re-birth out of self-loathing, the regaining of "my power" out of the overwhelming experience of fleshly containment, the sense of that sacrifice of human energy (the god-energy in the self) which conflict in both the self and the warfare world encourages, and the need to end the conflict through a re-birth into the humble body, conscious of the life-giving energy of the sun:

> The realization that the whole visonary game was lost, came on me on a train leaving Kyoto — at which point I started weeping and sobbing that I was still alive in a body that was going to die . . . [7]

In discussion with Robert Creeley at the Vancouver Conference, July 1963, he went further into this crucial typical situation:[8]

---

6 Paul Carroll: *The Poem in Its Skin* 1958, p.101: letter from Ginsberg, August 1966.
7 Allen Ginsberg: *Mystery in the Universe* 1965, (interview with Edward Lucie-Smith).
8 Robert Creeley: *Contexts of Poetry* — with Allen Ginsberg — *Audit* Vol. V/No. 1, Spring 1968.

11

... the last time I wrote was on a train to Kyoto and Tokyo. I suddenly had a great seizure of realization, on a whole bunch of levels. I was thinking of a poetic problem... also, about an emotional problem which was just resolving itself. And I was suddenly having feelings for the first time, certain kinds of feelings for the first time in about half a year. I was feeling something that had been growing and growing and growing and all of a sudden appeared to me on that train. So I had to get it then because I knew in an hour when I got to Tokyo I'd be all up in Tokyo — and I'd be having other feelings, or going back to material problems of arranging things. But here I had that moment... That's what I don't understand about your writing, what happens to you if you suddenly realize something — do you have to arrange your paper? What do you do then, you lose it!

Poetry, therefore, is a matter of finding the form of survival through which to offer hope, to the prohetic poet's audience: passages from a BBC interview in 1965 provide the connections between form and survival. The poem under discussion is "Magic Psalm" (1960):

The mind provides some kind of continuity, you know; all you have got to do is write down the sensuous data that you are apprehending at the moment... I trust that in time the data around me, the stimuli around me, and my own organism, will react in a way which will have form... All you've got to do is look at a very complicated model of the protoplasm or the DNA that they have built, and you see that it is like a big complicated reaction, and you can't exactly tell at first because it is much too complicated, but it does have a definite structure because it was built of chemicals that react symmetrically anway, and every reaction we have is a symmetrical reaction if you look at it close enough through an electron microscope...

Ginsberg's trust in his self, in the formal capacities of the self's body and in the universality of expressive feelings is not taken on mystical and vague belief: it is firmly based in Gestalt theory and in those structural truths about the form of organic life which underlie every religion. He is a profoundly traditional poet, therefore, and his contemporaneity lies in his urgent cry for the necessary renewal of a tradition which has been lost: that sense of our need to create what Blake calls "the human form divine", the four-fold son of man, which is present also in Whitman's "Laved in the flood of your bliss, o soul". The aim is pleasure, not self-torment, and poetry as a book of love:

> Whitman expresses this desire to be touched, it's probably a universal desire, that everybody who picks up his book wants to be touched. In other words, the desire to be touched intimately is very basic to the whole human organism, but it is being suppressed by everybody, and repressed . . .
> It turns out that the human organism, human beings, mammals, need, as part of their food, human contact — which is to say contact of skin to skin, the contact of meat to meat, the libidinous sexual and real emotional love chemical. It is not an intellectual thing. It is not an arbitrary thing. It is something built right into the chemical structure of the being. So unlike cold-war theorists and unlike hard policy theorists, who go all the way up the wrong track, it turns out that one of the basic necessities both for the babe to survive at all and for society also to survive is tenderness. Tenderness meaning the feeling that comes from skin to skin, giving that little thrill of acceptancy back and forth.

Ginsberg is able to offer and receive that tenderness internationally, both in his person and his poetry. In "Magic Psalm" he tests his ability to reject the tradition of an unhuman God of universal energy in order to discover the human divine form of energy — the four-fold son of man:

> I was exploring the possibilities of non-human paranoid religious urge, going imaginatively to the limits to see what would happen if I got out there; and I got out there, and I found a great cold inhuman universe, and I said: well all right, I'm God and this is not the universe I wish to create. I want to create my human universe. I want to live in the human universe.

It is the message of the end of Blake's "Jerusalem" and the content of Olson's poetry and essays; it is a thoroughly contemporary desire to create the human epic on a global basis of an entirely non-authoritarian ecology. But the verbal forms are difficult to find; the best account of the problem Ginsberg provides in some extended notes in *The Second Coming*, July 1961. He describes his "method" as the transciption of the "cornerless mystery" of his mind "in a form most nearly representing its actual 'occurence' . . . by means of spontaneous irrational juxtaposition of sublimely related fact". Poetry is an act of discovery:

> one must verge on the unknown, write toward the truth hitherto unrecognizable of one's own sincerity, including the unavoidable beauty of doom, shame and embarrassment, that very area of personal selfrecognition (detailed individual is universal remember) which formal conventions, internalized, keep us from discovery in ourselves & others — For if we write with an eye to what the poem should be (has been), and do not get lost in it, we will never discover anything new about ourselves in the process of actually writing on the table, and we lose the chance to live in our works,
> & make habitable the new world which every man may discover in himself, if he lives — which is life itself, past present and future.
> Thus the mind must be trained, i.e. let loose, freed — to deal with itself as it actually is, and not to impose on itself, or its poetic artefacts, an arbitrary preconceived pattern . . . The only pattern of value or interest in poetry is in the solitary, individual pattern peculiar to the poet's moment & the poem *discovered* in the mind & in the process of writing it out on the page, as notes, transcriptions, — reproduced in the fittest accurate form, at the time of composition . . . Mind is shapely, art is shapely.

After an exposure of American academic limitations, he quotes William Burroughs — "Any man who does not labour to make himself obsolete is not worth his salt" and indicates his own lineage: he cites Crane, Lorca, Biblical structures, Shelley, Apollinaire, Artaud, Myakovsky, Pound, Williams, Smart, Melville's *Pierre,* and "the spirit and illumination of Rimbaud". The enemy is "the false Jews from Columbia who have lost the memory of the Shekinah and are passing for middle class":

> The only poetic tradition is the Voice out of the burning bush. The rest is trash, and will be consumed.

But the Voice has its prosody, and what has been called by the academics "incoherent", both in "Howl" and in the writings of

Kerouac, is a formal prosody. The sleeve note for the recording of "Kaddish" delineats the prosodic structuring of the poem as an extension of forms in "The Change", and the actual reading shows that the form is also a system of notations for performance. Ginsberg describes the result with care:

> In the midst of the broken consciousness of mid twentieth century suffering anguish of separation from my own body and its natural affinity of feeling its own self with all self, I was instinctively seeking to reconstitute that blissful union which I experienced so rarely I took it to be supernatural and gave it holy Name thus made it hymn laments of longing and litanies of triumphancy of Self over the mind-illusion mechano-universe of un-feeling Time in which I saw myself my own mother and my very nation trapped desolate our worlds consciousness homeless and at war except for the original trembling of bliss in breast and belly of every body that nakedness rejected in suits of fear that familiar defenseless living hurt self which is myself same as all others abandoned scared to our own unchanging desire for each other. These poems almost unconscious to confess the beatific human fact, the language intuitively chosen as in trance and dream, the rhythm rising thru breath from belly and breast, the hymn completed in tears, the movement of the physical poetry demanding and receiving decades of life while chanting Kaddish the names of Death in many mind-worlds the self seeking the Key to life found at last in our Self.

In 1960, Ginsberg's international tenderness was not overtly political:

> people are beginning to see that the Kingdom of Heaven is within them, instead of thinking it's outside, up in the sky and that it can't be here on earth! It's time to seize power in the Universe, that's what I say — that's my "political statement". Time to seize power over the entire Universe. Not merely over Russia or America — seize power the moon — take the sun over. [9]

In 1963 he picketed in the San Francisco anti-Madame Nhu demonstration — "the first time I've taken a political stand" — but his sign read in part: "Till his humanity awakes says Blake /I am here saying seek mutual surrender tears/ That there be no more hell in

15

Vietnam / That I not be in hell here in the street/ War is black magic . . ." [10] Mutual surrender was the only answer to mutual bankruptcy. In 1965 he attempted, with some success, to deflect the Hell's Angels from disrupting Californian peace demonstrations against the war, and provided instructions on "How to make a March / Spectacle", as well as an address to the Angels themselves (reprinted in *Liberation*, January 1966):

> The parade can be made into an exemplary spectacle on how to handle situations of anxiety and fear/threat
> (such as Spectre of Hells Angels or Spectre of Communism)
> To manifest by concrete example, namely the parade itself, how to change war-psychology and surpass, go over, the habit-image-reaction of fear/violence.

The appeal to the Angels to realize their own "Anxiety Paranoia" did not, of course, work beyond the immediate situation ("All separate identities are bankrupt — Square, beat, Jews, negros, Hell's Angels, Communist and American"). But from this point on, in American and Europe, and in India through the new younger poets, Ginsberg has been unavoidably political in the most revolutionary way: "the revolt of the personal. Warsaw San Francisco Calcutta, the discovery of feeling". [11]

The fragment from "The Fall of America" (in *Pogamoggan 1*, 1964) warns America that the poor and the sacral energies of the human race will finally rise and defeat this world-conquering exploiter, and ends with a cry which now reads even more urgently and immediately than he must have intended in 1961:

> America, America, under the elms and Parks of Illinois, the anger, the anger, Beware!

Too many of Ginsberg's poems are anxiety patterns and not much else (a typical example is "On the Roof" in *Residu*, Spring 1965): his repetitious personality is probably encouraged by the demand for his work in little magazines. Even the figure of the Indian beggar reappears too frequently as an alibi of feeling and extreme bodily living. But this

---

9 The Sullen Art: Interviews with David Ossman (1963).
10 Ernie Barry: a Conversation with Allen Ginsberg — *City Lights Journal 2* 1964.
11 Allen Ginsberg — A Few Bengali Poets — *City Lights Journal 2* (1964).

man is a main character now in the *dramatis personae* of his political and religious life, and beautifully present in "A Writing (May 1963)" in *Gnaoua,* Spring 1964 — a short lyrical poem embodying this skeletal image of the basic, poverty-stricken, visibly decaying human urge to go on living. The rhythms are firm and there are no attempts at being funny or self-consciously ecstatic. The paraphernalia of self — lost identify cards, the pressure of masses felt in India — are focused in this basic man, about whom all Ginsberg's poems seem to have been moving. He is there in the Calcutta Journals (printed in *Intrepid* 5, 6 and 10) as a terrifying instance of ultimate man to who tenderness and aid must be offered:

> We all under Kali's foot or in Shiva's Bhang or/chillam high ganja reverie foreboding and dry mouth . . .
> . . . nothing less than death or /More than life possible in this here Coney Universe that repeats its possible Self over and over all the same boat and corpse returning cow /Shape moo . . .

And he is there as a leper in "Describe: The Rain on Dasawamedhu" (in *Planet News,*) once again as the instance of Kali's rule. Poetry cannot be obsolete while this lives to refute the social aims of the poet:

> a social place for the soul to exist manifested in this world. By soul I mean that which differs from thing, i.e. person, — not mere mental consciousness — but feeling bodily consciousness.[12]

On the one hand, in Ginsberg's world, his own nation expends "its deepest energies in wars . . . against the yellow and other races", and on the other, expands the poverty of the world: "prosperity . . . really a great psychic hoax. a mirage of electric mass-hypnosis, the real horror, the real evil latent in America from the days of Poe to the Days of Burroughs." So that beyond the political lies personal survival in order to speak out in poetry:

> Finally it becomes too much to fight. But the stakes are too great to lose — the possession of one's feelings intact.

The basic outrage is "to live in a country which supposedly

---

12 Allen Ginsberg: Back to the Wall — *Times Literary Supplement,* August 6, 1964.

dominates the entire planet and to be responsible for the outrages of one's own country!" His tenderness is endangered in battle against the exhausting forces of "the military machine non-person rage that dominates the thinking feeling massmedia family life publishing life universities business and budgetary government of my nation". Poetry opposes the Unreal and its manipulatory centres of power: but in the fight "how can the soul endure?" — "what happens to real bodily human feelings confronted with inhuman response? The feelings and the response become seeming unreal. Total disorganization". Poetry must be "the renaissance of individual sensibility carried thru the vehicle of individualized metrics", and that is exactly why the police attack the avant-garde. In "Kansas City to St. Louis", one of the long sections of the poem on "These States" (*TV Baby Poems*, 1967), Ginsberg puts the problem in its most urgent form: the condition of power in America.

He shows the culture of the people of the Middle West as a treachery called "We the People" seething inside a vitalistic programme of terror: Fulton —

> where Churchill rang down the curtain
> > on Consciousness
> and set a chill which overspread the world
> > one icy day in Missouri
> > not far from the Ozarks —
> Provincial ears heard Spenglerian Iron
> > Terror Pronouncement
> Magnificent Language, they said,
> > for county ears —

The lyrical impassioned movement — Ginsberg at his finest — moves towards his own position:

> The hero surviving his own murder,
> > his own suicide, his own
> > addiction, surviving his own
> poetry, surviving his own
> > disappearance from the scene —
> returned in new faces, shining
> > through the tears of new eyes . . .

> ... the wanderer returns
> from the west with his Powers
> the Shaman with his beard
> in full strength,
> the longhaired Crank with subtle humorous voice
> enters city after city
> to kiss the eyes of your high school sailors
> and make laughing Blessing
> for a new Age in America ...

Planet News is a record of his right to be that laughing prophet. Today his poetry is a continuous record of space-time travel in the Cold War. He is a media man, fearful of global electronic communications networks but trying to employ them for his own ends of humane communication — the condition of every peaceful revolutionary. Ginsberg's voice and image are available internationally in the flesh, on film, on records, in books, on posters and on television. With the other major American poets of our time — Williams, Pound, Zukofsky, Olson, Duncan — he is making the continuous open-ended epic which will end with his life: the information programme for these men is endlessly exploratory, continually. forming, disintegrating and re-forming. Ginsberg's scroll is not encyclopaedic, as it is in Duncan and Olson — he does not have their manic desire for the inclusive myth of all myths, the geography of all history. His self-centredness does make for a certain monotony of urgency, despair, reiteration of disasters and tyrants, and disgust with his alternately melancholic and exuberant self. *Planet News* is the book of a busy social man agonised in private, a traveller recorder who has vowed to maintain his impressions in notebooks and on tape. The poems, "journal notations" and journal compositions have a vitality of mani need to define, to master complexity and universality, and to keep off self-distrust, despair and impotence.

Ginsberg's poems of the Sixties originate largely from travel, either in a car driving across America or in the space-time of the airplane, the most recent area of meditation over the earth. But he is still the lonely man of *Empty Mirror*, (1960) the book of his earliest poems, and still as alert and compassionate as "the radars revolve in their Solitude" ("New York to San Fran"). His self-revelatory need for vulnerability

19

has made him an action poet, covering the area of discovery and exposure with immediate experience until it yields, with luck and ability, the action of the times. His popularity is part of a larger vision, in America and beyond, of the anarchist principles of decentralization, personal autonomy and anti-authoritarianism which are the major action of the world today. Ginsberg's presence guarantees a recognition that national identity and character armouring are mere blockages of the rotten past. His aim, as he said on the occasion of his ICA reading in London in 1967, is **"the possibility of harmony and peacefulness between generations"**, but he is acutely aware of the limitations of poetry's white magic against the black magic of the warring nation states. It is the ironic core of "Wichita Vortex Sutra", instanced by the "magic wafer" Ike took from Dulles —**"an evidence of white Christian Black Magic conspiracy against no "Christian World"**, as he told Paul Carroll.

Ginsberg has become a world-traveller through his desire to ascertain what forces are available against black magic and chaos — the ancient possible tradition of unity between men, and between men and their universe:

> There is a tradition of the transcendental in America, but no contact with the sources. But it's now possible, by jet-plane, to have realistic contact with the sources you fantasize upon.[13]

The "human universe" is his concern; he discovers, as Blake knew very well, that you must invent it out of the experience of disaster, the furnaces of Los's regeneration. But there is a part of Ginsberg which yearns for the Void, for the end of struggle, in the knowledge that possessions are a fetish and the possession of life the worst of all. In the sections of the journals in *Boss*, Summer 1966, he dreams of T.S. Eliot **"in a haunted house"**, reading his poems as if it is all **"empty now finally — no meaning to all that earlier intense seriousness"** — and he adds: **"So that's what happened"**. A second dream (Saigon 1962) warns him **"not to believe in Poetry — . . . not to hang on to anything at all"**. He must have well understood Ezra Pound's self-denunciation and remorse when they met in Italy in 1967. He praises the *Cantos* as **"the theatre, the record, of flux of consciousness"** and of **"the magnanimity of the desire to manifest coherent perceptions in**

---

13 *Mystery in the Universe* — ibid.
14 "A Conversation between Ezra Pound and Allen Ginsberg" *Evergreen Review 55, 1968.*

language", and as "a working model of your mind":

> I'm a Buddhist Jew whose perceptions have been strengthened by the series of practical exact language models scattered through the *Cantos* like stepping stones . . . [14]

It is as if he were reassuring Pound against that cosmic uselessness of poetry which part of himself acknowledges. Their humilities meet, but Ginsberg goes again into the world, as the prophet in the Ike-Nixon-McCarthy-Kennedy-Johnson-Nixon sequence of chaos, the poet who renews the transcendental in America by injections from the East and discoveries about inner space. "Remarks on Leary's Politics of Ecstasy" (*Village Voice*, December 12, 1968) gives his most recent cultural context:

> "Ourselves caught in the giant machine are conditioned to its terms, only holy vision or technological catastrophe or revolution break "the mind-forg'd manacles".

The tension is his poetry forms between acceptance and revolt, between acknowledgement of Kali — the goddess of *Planet News* and "Ankor Wat" — and the need for action poetry. Kali's ritual requires human sacrifice but she finally transcends conflict of forces. The gnostic equality of good and evil is a moral duality which Ginsberg opposes, and his concern is more with the gnostic Ouroboros — definition, defense, the enclosure of body-mind elements which threaten to overwhelm the self, especially in the chaotic environment of this decade — and with the yin-yang circle which is bipartite, dynamic, complimentary and polar energies in a state, not of conflict but of creative polarity. Although he uses the web of evil connections as a constant image for his world, he does not appear to believe, gnostically, that evil is at the origin of things, although its demiurges abound in his environment. He knows enough about the ancient relationship between life and death as sources of all evil to be wary of rejecting ancient religions of any kind. But he has little of either William Burroughs' sceptical misanthropy or Jack Kerouac's melancholic exuberance for physically demonstrated living, boisterous and verbally manic, as if to ward off impending corruption.

Unlike Olson and Duncan, Ginsberg moves through comparative mythology, not by libraries, but by travel to source countries: he is in touch, physically, as well as in the sense of erudition, with the myths that inform global culture. He knows that love and conjunction are partly formed from struggle, but he is exhausted and exasperated by the lack-love society which sets up endless internal and external conflicts which it has no means either to eliminate or calm, the society of Burroughs' novels. Again and again in *Planet News* the irony lies in his American nationality — a member of a nation notorious for its aggressive military and economic predations against the globe. His own sexuality — ambivalent, but weighed towards homosexuality — is itself a state of conflict in such a society of masculinity hang-ups, the environment exploded by Mailer's *Why Are We in Vietnam?*. (1967) One cannot always remain a private being and Ginsberg has no desire to be other than public in his prophetic stance, despite his recurrent desire for privacy —

> **Always the telephone linked to all the hearts of the world beating at once,**

as he says in "I am a Victim of Telephone". To be both a public figure and an innocent man is Ginsberg's aim. His remorse and self-disgust, too frequently and similarly offered in his poems, are a result of a gap between egoism and humility in the messianic poet who seeks *praxis* as well as enlightenment, poetic form as well as autobiographical relaxation, private love as well as media and crowd control. His particular synthesis, in poetics and ideas, has been evolved to combat the "emotional plague" of our time. In "Reflections on the Mantra" *(Back to Godhead* 1.3, 1966) he describes his use of the mantra with which he begins his readings and which is part of the structure of his recent poems. It is in the tradition of phonetic symbolism, found in Egyptian, Gnostic and Mithraic rituals, which holds that the vibrations of a syllable are cosmic breath modulations and tune the sounder in to elemental power. The Hindu version uses *om* or *aum* — a is beginning, u is transition, m is end or deep sleep — and Ginsberg incorporates it into his own purpose with no sense of esoteric tricks and borrowings. As he says, the short repeated verbal formula is common to Negro spirituals, Tennyson, the Rolling Stones and Gertrude Stein, as a physical evocation of "a kind of magic language". Repeating the word may induce self-communion and raise up latent feeling, making visible and audible the hidden self:

subjective sensation ... fixing the mind on one point, focussing and deepening in one spot is a classical method of yoga meditation.

Ginsberg first heard his Hare Krishna mantram in Allahabad: "the song was impressed on my own memory. It came back after many adventures". Its effect is part of that expanding of consciousness which he has practised since his adolscence. His journals for 1952, when he was 26 (Birth 3, Book 1, 1960) record his peyote experiences in Paterson — a sense of unity ("Heavens, the universe is in order"), his paranoia, the mystery of being:

> I have to find, among other things, a new god for the universe. I'm tired of the old ones, they mean too many things from other times and people. Also amazing how my real fixation on T or anything returns to this wonder at the world of solid substance & stops simply gazing at appearance, with scant regard for telos or final mechanics ...

> However it strikes me that perhaps I and Williams (W.C.) in a radius of miles around — stand so solidly on terra firma/admiring ...

I would like to write a poem. Divine Poem on the physical world ... Out of his experience of a peculiarly American drug (used originally by the original Americans) he gains a knowledge that is still with him:

> Peyote is not God — but is a powerful force — can see, if everybody how they would organize their lives once every year, communicating with each other — what spiritual violence that day — what secrets revealed — family secrets, not big mystical riddles, which are after all palpable and easy to see just by staring outward into the obvious infinity of the sky —
> ... problem of matter & infinity and origin of Creation to be assessed and thought into without the aid of reason or science, but with the inner imagination ... impasses of imagination ... returns the mind to the fact that looking into the sky see the solid endless

heaven existing out there ... going up from us (our glance) endlessly ...

When the mind reaches that solid impossible wall it knows it's off in a meaningless series of ideas and must return ...

That essential commonsense, even utilitarian, use of expanded consciousness is palpably American, and part of a more general discovery process in this century. "Remarks on Leary's Politics of Ecstasy" places it in a field which includes Whitman, Ginsberg's Blake, and Pound's "With usura the line grows thick", but also Blake's visionary Harvard scholar S. Foster Damon, to whom Virgil Thomson once gave peyote, William James's *Varieties of Religious Experience* in which the Harvard scholar includes "shamanistic chemical visions", his student Gertrude Stein who "experimented in alteration of consciousness through mindfulness of language", William Burroughs who expanded his Harvard anthropology studies to include drug-shamanism experiments, and Timothy Leary's Harvard experiments with inner space. In the 1940s the North Pacific poets Snyder, Spicer and Duncan (who had met Leary in 1948), together with Kerouac and Neal Cassady, wrote with **"the new consciousness"** which itself can be traced back **"through old gnostic texts, visions, artists and shamans; it is the consciousness of our ground nature suppressed and desecrated"**. Aldous Huxley, Charlie Parker, Thelonious Monk and Dizzy Gillespie are drawn into that resurrection of the body which Norman Brown delineates in his two books and in his essay on the uses of Marx, "From Politics to Metapolitics", delivered at Harvard in 1967. He, too, uses Blake, and also the Harvard poet and philosopher of the American Renaissance, Emerson:

Emerson used to say, There is only one Man
After Emerson, what happened, on the American continent, to this intuition?[15]

Ginsberg's work, in the light of Brown's essay, appears as part of what he terms "utopian engineering", along with all the other figures in this American line.

Today the politics of genocide are countered by the politics of biochemical and meditational consciousness changes, a counter-politics of release. But it is also a return. The messianic task for any man, not only Ginsberg, is "accelerated evolution", a psychological revolution whose consciousness changes involve "the immediate mutation of social and economic forms". Blake's "mind-forg'd manacles" and Urizen's torment of Los can be ended, Ginsberg claims, by "holy vision or technological catastrophe or revolution". Given the conditioned reflexes of the manipulated masses of the earth, the messianic task is to inhibit those reflexes. *Planet News* is news of how far the beginnings of the revolution have advanced. Against destructive technology of weapons and money, the technology of psychedelics offers what Burroughs calls a regulator, a method of opposing the conspiracy without being destroyed oneself. It is exactly Ginsberg's aim also. **"From Bratislava to San Francisco"**, he says, youth responds to **"ancient body rhythms beat out thru airwaves in electric mantric Rock"** and **"ingests shamanic elixirs to recover consciousness of planetary Archtypes"**. The return and the recovery are one.

Ginsberg, through his poetry, has become the image of the possibility of recovery and return, and as Paul Zweig observes, "in payment, he has received the gift of love. Now nothing human is foreign to him". [16] He can contact any man — one of his most moving writings shows him moving easily and tenderly among the holymen in Calcutta, identifying with emaciated beggars, and realizing the helplessness of poetry, **"the vast space filled with giant stars"**, and the "great crash of buildings and planets" breaking "the walls of language". Under such stress the poet does not **"close the dream in the old known box"** and yield to "a hollow dream dying to finish its all too famous misery":

> — leave immortality for another to suffer like a fool.
> **not get stuck in a corner of the Universe**
> **sticking morphine in the arm and eating meat.** [17]

"Television was a Baby Crawling Toward that Deathchamber" is as complete an exposure of the conditions of survival as we have from any winter in the Sixties. It, and not "Wichita Vortex Sutra", is the core of

---

15 *Caterpillar 1*, 1967
16 Paul Zweig: A Music of Angels — *The Nation*, March 10, 1969.
17 *Calcutta Journals, Intrepid 10* 1968 (c.f. Allen Ginsberg: *Indian Journals*, 1970).

Planet News because its information is inclusive, and consistently dislocated and reassembled into an action. The ideogram of Pound is fused into the Hart Crane telescopic image and Blake's prophetic "Jerusalem" tactics (the multipresence of contemporaneity within prophetic universality); the result is a rhetoric of highlighted word-ideas which resist the logic of linear cause and effect structures. The poem is a mobile of urgency, as full of grotesques as Nathanael West and as black in its humour. The network of black magic controls is fully given — police, government, media — and "the Man-God", Ginsberg's version of the four-fold son of man or Stevens's "major man", is postulated. The poem emerges as a weapon against tyranny, an announcement of possible rebirth out of the Armaggedon of the media. It is a monstrous book of American power, a diagnosis of the realm of Kali, and a parody of pervertedly incarnated energy. *Planet News* ends with "Pentagon Exorcism", a ritual against the centre of black magic, the Pentagon; and the whole book is in a sense a ritual exorcism composed by an intelligence on its *periplum* of discovery.

But besides this major poem stands Ginsberg's great poem of that unit he experienced in 1952 in Paterson — here in 1967 it is in Wales: "Wales Visitation" is an accurate description, under LSD, of human oneness with the earth, a marvellous ecology — "the widom of earth relations", "extended motion", "balance", "one solemn wave", "no imperfection", "grassy mandalas", "the wind's Kaballah", a "symmetry" of "particulars". Ginsberg's poetry and prophecy moves out from the ineffable security of experiencing the earth as part of a human universe, not in gradiose theory alone but through "a blind rock covered with mist ferns" and the "teeming ferns equisitely swayed along a green grag". The agony of *"The Change"* is converted into the true pleasure of *"Wales Visitation"*, his "Divine Poem on the physical world".